DO TREES HAVE MOTHERS?

DO TREES HAVE MOTHERS?

WRITTEN AND ILLUSTRATED BY CHARLES BONGERS

*Written and illustrated under
the watchful eye of Nuts,
the original tree planter.*

*Eighty percent of the
time Nuts forgets where
the acorns are stashed!*

dotreeshavemothers.com | @dotreeshavemothers

Text and illustrations copyright © 2022 Charles Bongers

02 03 04 05 – 26 25 24 23 22

Douglas and McIntyre (2013) Ltd.
P.O. Box 219, Madeira Park, BC, V0N 2H0
douglas-mcintyre.com

Edited by Sarah Harvey
Book illustration and design by Charles Bongers
Printed and bound in Canada
Printed with soy-based ink on paper certified by the
  Forest Stewardship Council®

Douglas and McIntyre acknowledges the support of the Canada Council for the Arts, the Government of Canada, and the Province of British Columbia through the BC Arts Council.

Library and Archives Canada Cataloguing in Publication

Title: Do trees have mothers? / Charles Bongers.
Names: Bongers, Charles, author.
Identifiers: Canadiana (print) 20210366672 | Canadiana
  (ebook) 20210366680 | ISBN 9781771623254 (hardcover) |
  ISBN 9781771623261 (EPUB)
Subjects: LCSH: Forest ecology–Juvenile literature. |
  LCSH: Forests and forestry–Juvenile literature. | LCSH: Trees–
  Ecology–Juvenile literature. | LCSH: Trees–Juvenile literature.
Classification: LCC QH541.5.F6 B66 2022 | DDC j577.3–dc23

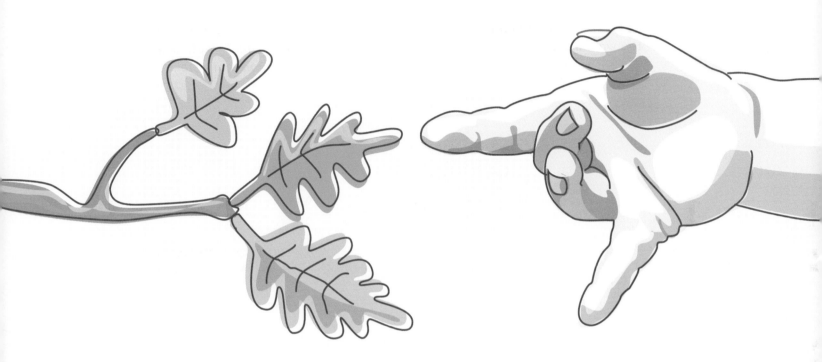

For my children Emma, Shawn and Andrea, with all my love and energy.

Hi. My name is Nuts, and I would
like to tell you a story about how,

just like puppies, piglets, kittens,

and ducklings, trees have mothers too.

Every spring, baby trees

pop up all over the forest.

With the help of their mothers,
they grow up to be big and strong.

Mother trees are easy to spot.
They're the tall ones in the
middle of all their babies.

When baby trees get thirsty,

they can call out to their mothers.

And when they get sick, their mothers
can make them feel better too.

Mother trees teach their
babies through their roots.

They can even warn them when
there are pesky bugs around.

Mother trees help others by cleaning the air and water.

They create flowers so bees can make honey,

and they grow tasty fruits and nuts too.

At the end of the day, mother trees

make safe, cozy, warm beds to sleep in.

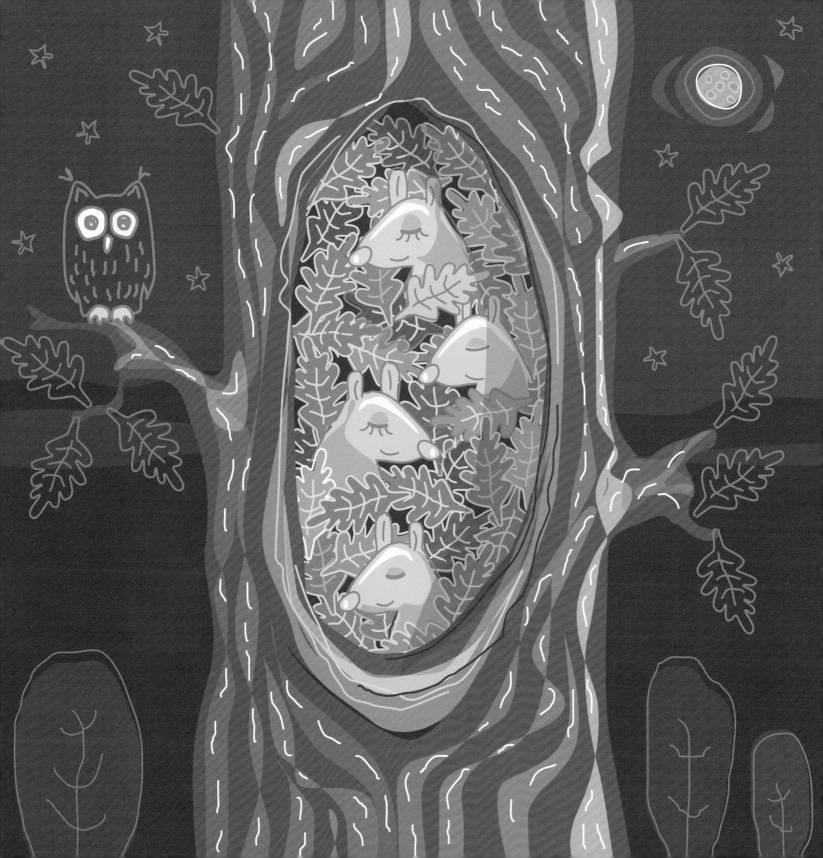

So next time you see a baby
tree, say hi, and remember,
trees really do have mothers.

There are many research studies that show how "mother trees" connect with the forest around them.

REFERENCES:

The mother tree:
Simard, Suzanne. "The Mother Tree Project." https://mothertreeproject.org/.

Trees can help each other:
Simard, Suzanne, David A. Perry, Melanie D. Jones, David D. Myrold, Daniel M. Durall, and Randy Molina. "Net Transfer of Carbon Between Ectomycorrhizal Tree Species in the Field." *Nature* 388, no. 6642 (1997): 579–82. https://doi.org/10.1038/41557.

Trees learn and remember:
Gagliano, Monica, Michael Renton, Martial Depczynski, and Stefano Mancuso. "Experience Teaches Plants to Learn Faster and Forget Slower in Environments Where It Matters." *Oecologia* 175, no. 1 (2014): 63–72. https://doi.org/10.1007/s00442-013-2873-7.

Trees communicate with each other:
Gagliano, Monica, Stefano Mancuso, and Daniel Robert. "Towards Understanding Plant Bioacoustics." *Trends in Plant Science* 17, no. 6 (2012): 323–25. https://doi.org/10.1016/j.tplants.2012.03.002.

Rhodes, Christopher J. "The Whispering World of Plants." *Science Progress* 100, no. 3 (2017): 331–37. https://doi.org/10.3184/003685017x14968299580423.

Maffei, Massimo and Wilhelm Boland. "The Silent Scream of the Lima Bean." Paper presented at Chemical Ecology: The Variety of Secondary Metabolites, Jena, Germany, June 2007. https://doi.org/10.13140/2.1.4887.6806.

TREES ARE OUR ANCIENT ANCESTORS THAT
HAVE FOUND A MORE PEACEFUL WAY OF BEING.
- SHAWN BONGERS -